Jan Pieńkowski

The Monster Pet

Rigby

A Harcourt Achieve Imprint

www.Rigby.com
1-800-531-5015

Five little monsters have a pet.

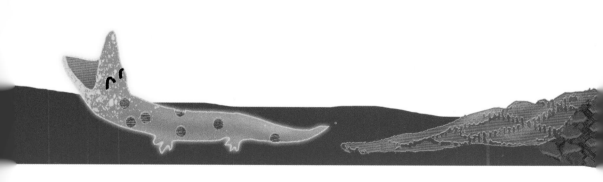

It hasn't had its supper yet.

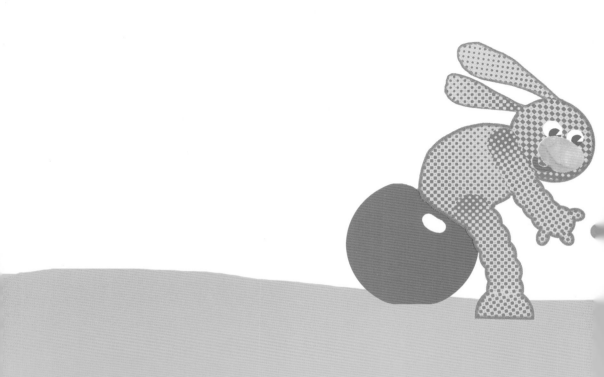

The yellow monster gives it peas.

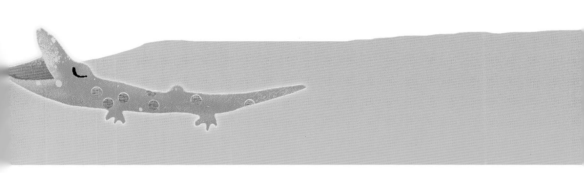

The purple monster gives it cheese.

The orange monster cooks a stew.

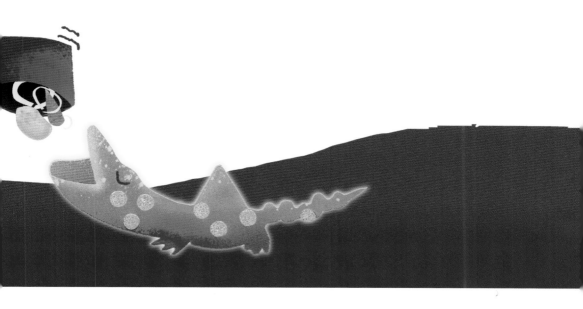

The little red monster tries shampoo.

The big blue monster gives it cake.

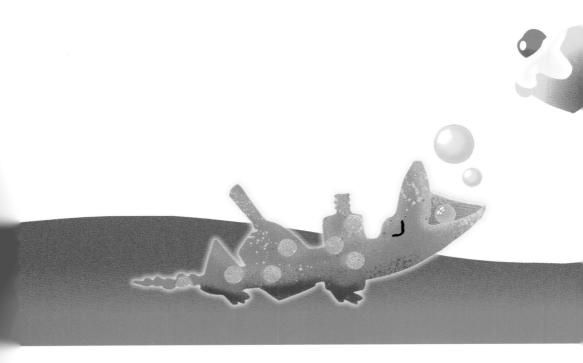

They go to sleep . . .

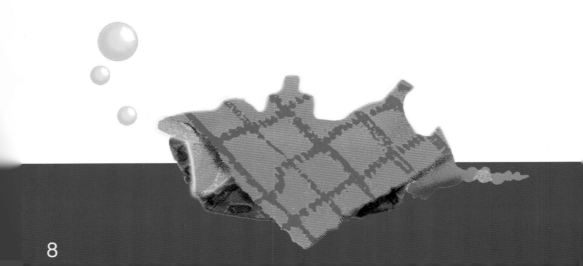

. . . it stays awake.

Five little monsters have a pet.

It hasn't had its breakfast yet.

The orange monster's lost his hat.

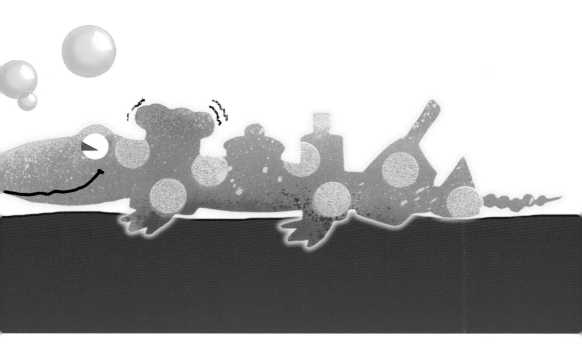

The purple monster's lost his bat.

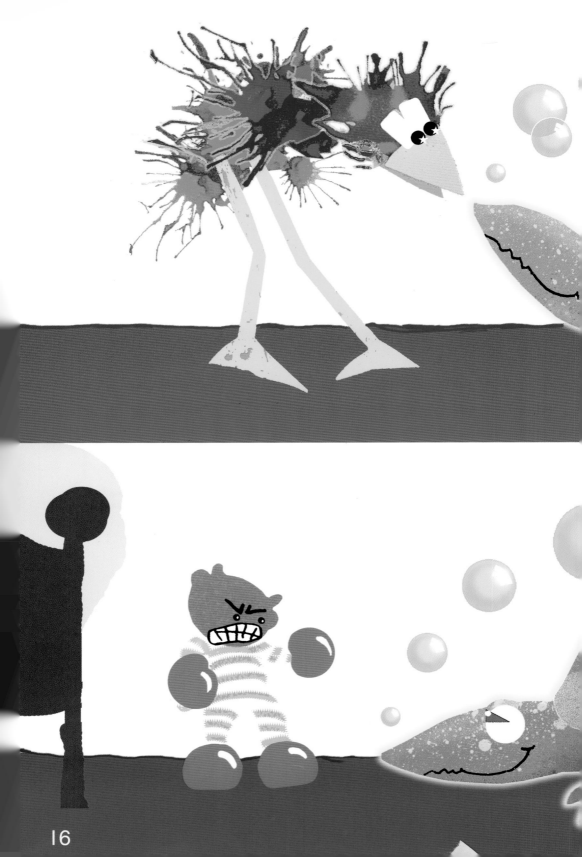

The big blue monster's lost his coat.

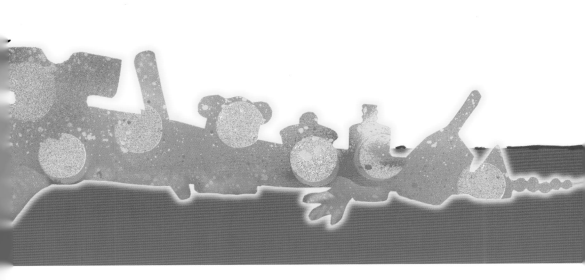

The little red monster's lost his boat.

18

The yellow monster's lost his ball.

Who do you think has got them all?

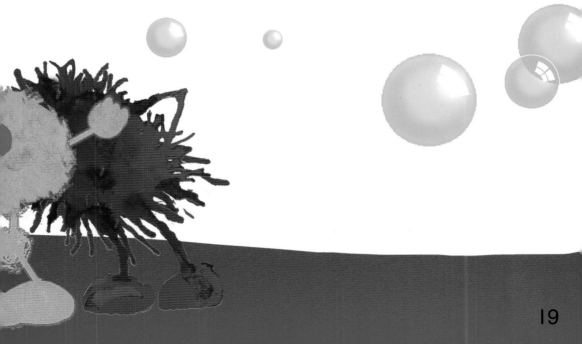

Five little monsters have a pet.

It hasn't had its dinner . . .

. . . yet .